RD

ans

spital

London S.E

Kenya
—

...per Econom. Research
Bureau

...roceedings of the
Technical session Agric
Research Conference

...Publications Education
...n East Africa

Italie
—
(3)
Recueil de
Législation
—

F.A.O

VINTAGE EPHEMERA

VINTAGE EPHEMERA

From the collection of
CAVALLINI & CO.

Brian D. Coleman

Photographs by William Wright

GIBBS SMITH
TO ENRICH AND INSPIRE HUMANKIND

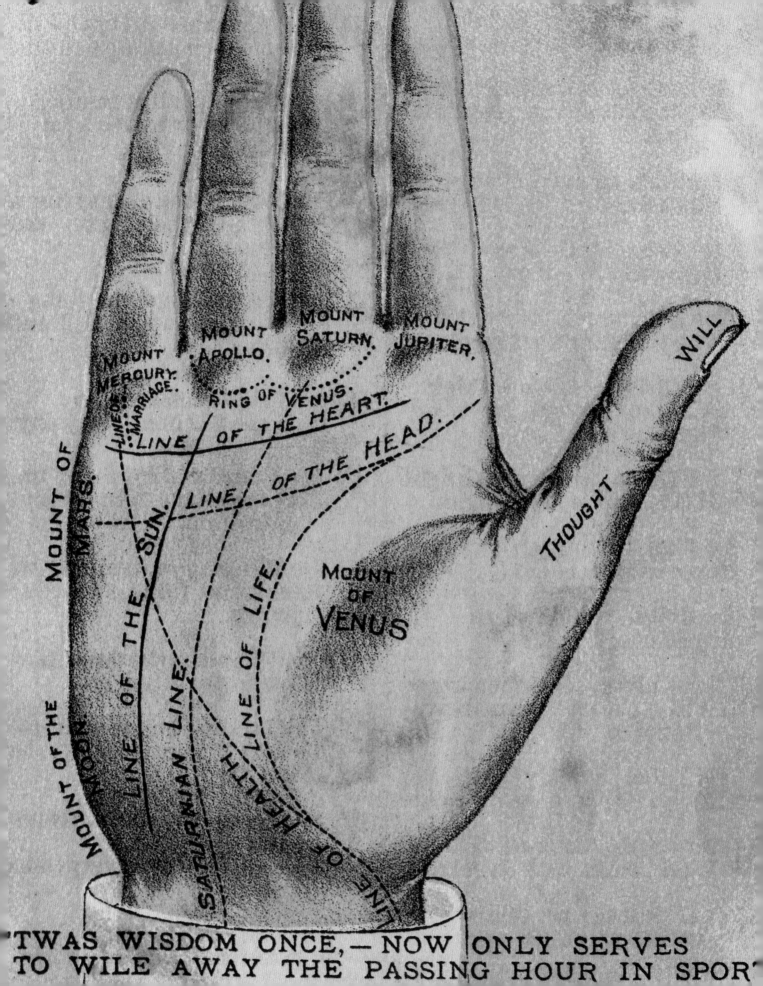

'TWAS WISDOM ONCE,—NOW ONLY SERVES
TO WILE AWAY THE PASSING HOUR IN SPORT

Contents

The dictionary defines ephemera as things that are important or useful for only a short time; items that were not meant to have lasting value. Maurice Rickards, who along with others formed the Ephemera Society in London in 1975, thought ephemera to be the "minor transient documents of everyday life." Ephemera was not meant to be preserved; it was created to meet the needs of the day and to be discarded once it had served its original purpose. Contrary to expectations, much of it was saved.

Ephemera is everywhere. Much of it comes from advertising and packaging. An example from my own life may begin to explain why people are drawn to these transient documents. Not too long ago, I made a cup of tea. While the tea was steeping, I looked at the tea bag tag. It possessed, to my mind, such good design that I didn't want to throw it away. So I saved it. At the time, I wasn't sure what I would do with it, but it caught my eye in a way that made me want to keep it. What to one person is a scrap of paper destined for the trash is to another a treasure. But these incidental scraps of paper can take on new meaning to a collector.

People are drawn to ephemera and choose to collect it for many reasons. Some collections simply reflect people's likes. They like dogs, so they collect dog-themed ephemera. My childhood baseball card collection reflects my early love of sports. Some ephemera is collected to evoke memories of a specific event or time. A saved ticket stub or playbill can transport you back to a special concert or show. Greeting cards, postcards, and correspondence are saved for the same reason. The appeal of certain pieces of ephemera lies in their design quality, like my tea bag tag. Yet another reason for assembling a collection is the desire to travel back in time and connect to another era. Historically minded collectors may choose to focus on World War II memorabilia or a particular World's Fair or Exposition. The desire to collect often encompasses more than one of these reasons.

Ephemera takes on added significance precisely because of the unique, idiosyncratic meanings that we attach to it. What objectively is just a piece of paper is transformed by us into something much more powerful and personal. Because of that, what different people collect is as varied as their reasons for collecting. Collections can be organized by subject matter or by type of ephemera. Popular subject matters are entertainment, travel, education, cats, dogs, sports, and medicine. Trade cards, baggage labels, food wrappers and packaging, poster stamps, letterheads, and handbills are examples of frequently collected formats. A collection can be formed based on typography, a specific printing process such as letterpress or chromolithography, or a style such as Art Nouveau or Art Deco.

Collecting ephemera can be an inexpensive hobby, so its appeal is not just for the seasoned collector. Many ephemeral objects are available free: pamphlets, matchbooks, timetables, menus, business cards, and maps. The value lies in what the item means to the collector.

Beyond the world of collecting, ephemera has more uses. In the academic world, social and cultural historians sometimes refer to ephemera as part of material culture. Ephemera can give a picture of the past beyond what is found in the official record. Studying these documents of everyday life can explain the past and help us understand it in a more personal way than secondary sources such as history books have the ability to do. Business history becomes much more interesting when trade cards, letterheads, bills and receipts, and even paper bags are examined. With ephemera one can follow the changes and evolution in advertising or package design, for example. The study of ephemera shines a light on popular culture, local history, social life, and the history of printing. It can show how people of the past lived their lives.

The art world also embraces ephemera. Any history of graphic arts notes the importance of ephemera such as posters in the chronology of design. All these bits of paper have been given a new life and been put to use in the art of collage. Kurt Schwitters was an early-twentieth-century master of the genre. He used candy wrappers, magazine clippings, tickets, envelopes, playing cards, and price tags in his work. American artist Joseph Cornell used printed ephemera to great effect in his collages as both components and inspiration.

People's need to collect and connect has given ephemera a new life beyond its original purpose. For instance, my small collection of travel-themed ephemera—airline playing cards—illustrates the point. The cards date from the 1960s, when the airlines gave the decks free to passengers. The cards show the cities the airlines served and are splendid examples of mid-century design. To the student of history, they are evidence of a more generous time in air travel. For me, there is a sentimental attachment to the cards, as they came from a favorite aunt. One collection—many reasons for keeping it.

There is much to be learned and enjoyed from an appreciation of ephemera. Think back to the tea bag tag I saved. I could keep it with other items I've collected for their good design. Then again, maybe I'll put it to good use in a tea-themed collage. A small piece of ephemera with countless possibilities.

—Jan Grenci
Reference Specialist
Prints and Photographs Division
Library of Congress

The Story of Cavallini

The Cavallini archives began with a set of luggage labels I received when I was nine years old. In February of 1968, an envelope bearing a six-cent stamp arrived in the mail at my childhood home in Bellingham, Washington, containing eight paper luggage labels from around the world. The labels came from such disparate places as Mexico, Indonesia, Israel, and Nigeria. One came from a country that no longer exists. These labels were treasures, beautifully designed but ephemeral—destined to be attached to a suitcase that one day, worn, would be discarded. Preserving them and other paper artifacts became a passion of mine. Without realizing, I became a collector, stopping at the Salvation Army on my way home from school to sift through trade cards, outdated maps, movie magazines, and used postcards—all of them works of art in their own right. These pieces of paper illuminated the daily life of distant places and simpler times, and were my introduction to the world and history beyond my hometown.

Since then, the collection has grown enormously. From late-nineteenth-century souvenir postcards to European guidebooks, from hundred-year-old satirical prints to studies of landscapes, the collection includes imagery spanning four centuries and many thousands of miles. Pieces in the collection come from the rare print stores of London's Cecil Court, the flea markets of New York and Munich, antique fairs in California, and anyplace in between that might yield a gem. The archive contains English, French, and German encyclopedias from the eighteenth and nineteenth centuries, including the Bertuch editions, with their incredibly detailed depictions of the natural world. For many years I focused on acquiring botanical imagery, much of which originated in England in the late eighteenth to mid-nineteenth century. These painstakingly hand-colored illustrations are nearly living things themselves, infused with the personalities and idiosyncratic styles of the artisans who created them.

The Cavallini archives are the foundation of the company I established in 1989. Botanical prints from the collection were used to produce the company's first products—large-format calendars that were inspired by an art calendar that I bought in Perugia during a year of study in Italy. Today, the collection is the source of images for our latest generation of calendars and all of our other printed products. Most of our products are printed on Italian paper, supporting mills hundreds of years old in the country where my grandmother was born. I named the company after my grandmother's married name to commemorate her life and my family's ancestral ties to Italy. Today, Cavallini operates based on an old-fashioned model, with all aspects of the company under one roof. Our products are designed, hand-assembled, and hand-packed in South San Francisco by a small and dedicated team below the second-floor archives. In that way, the archive is not only a source for the products but also stands as a daily reminder of the origins of the company and its future.

It is an honor to celebrate Cavallini's 25th anniversary year with you through this publication. In that time, our collection of luggage labels alone has grown to number almost 4,000! These and all of the images in the archives continue to inspire and delight us, and it is our pleasure to share them with you here.

—Brad Parberry
Founder, Cavallini & Co.

From left: Sookie Koban, Director of Product Development, with Jennifer Chen, Creative Director, and Brad Parberry in the Cavallini archives. Collaborators for many years, the trio combs the collection daily for images to inspire new Cavallini products of the highest quality.

The Cavallini family in the warehouse at the Cavallini office in South San Francisco.

BANGKOK

DE MEXICO · AERONAVE

CATHAY

SPANNING THE ORIENT EV

Brad Parberry
3111 Lindbergh
Bellingham, WA   98225

RD CLASS   ag 23 al
CHANDISE

The first items in the
Cavallini archives: luggage
labels purchased by
Brad Parberry in 1968.

Various show
ribbons housed at
Cavallini & Co.

Various trade
cards, circa 1890.

Cats and dogs, owls, even cows and roosters—nothing captures our hearts and our attention better than a charming animal. Companies have been quick to capitalize on this since the nineteenth century, when animal-themed promotional trade cards were handed out. These ephemera, such as an 1884 trade card of a wise old owl reminding us that Boraxine was "better than soap," remain as endearing today as they were a century ago. And who could resist a 1910 stationery trade card of an earnest puppy staring straight into their eyes?

Cats and kittens were just as popular and often associated with more feminine pursuits such as sewing or knitting, as an 1865 trade card for Standard Sewing Machines demonstrates, with a parade of patriotic cats marching down the street. Barnyard animals were also used, as most Americans still lived on farms in the 1880s, and prize Jersey bulls and brown Leghorn roosters were proudly displayed on trade cards for the Domestic Sewing Machine Company. Lighthearted and amusing, animal-themed ephemera never loses its appeal.

Animals

We shall be at home at *April ...*

LOUIS WAIN
COPYRIGHT ENTD AT STAT HALL.

M. H. FIELDSTAD,
LEADING DEALER IN
DRY GOODS, HATS, CAPS,
And Groceries,
WELLS, MINN.

Selection of various owl objects and ephemera.

Facing: Postcard, Nurnburg, Germany, 1898.

Trade card for Geiger Bros., Newark, NJ, circa 1910.

Various new and vintage rubber stamps.

Nürnberg : Theo. Stroefer's Kunstverlag. Aquarell-Postkarte. Serie V. No. 5062.

Get your **Stationery** And **Printing** AT

GEIGER BROS.

77 Springfield Avenue.

TELEPHONE 324. NEWARK, N. J.

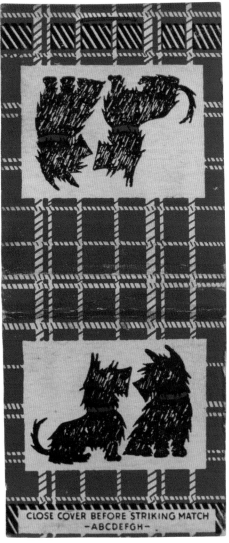

Postcard, printed
in Germany, 1905.

Matchbook,
American,
circa 1935.

Facing:
Postcard, printed
in Germany, 1908.

Second-prize
ribbon, Kennel
Club, Urbana,
IL, 1955.

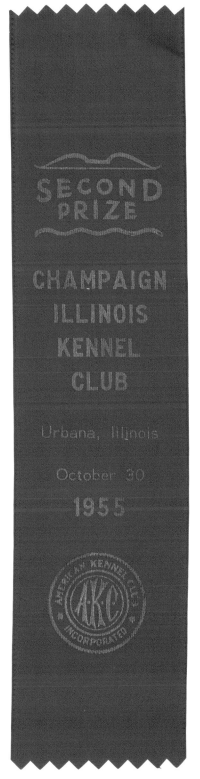

The Black Cat

November. 1896.

Silas F. Quigley — To Arrive.
Lewis Hopkins Rogers.

The Polar Magnet.
Philip Verrill Mighels.

Fitzhugh.
W. Macpherson Wiltbank.

The Passionate Snake.
Ella Higginson.

Professor Whirlwind.
Allen Quinan.

5

Facing:
Trade card,
Standard Sewing
Machine Co.,
Philadelphia,
PA, circa 1865.

Postcard, printed
in France, 1903.

This page:
Magazine,
The Black Cat,
Boston, MA,
November 1896.

The Great New York Bazaar.

GOTTSCHALK & LEDERMAN,
26 & 28
North Queen Street,
LANCASTER, PA.

J.

Various trade cards, circa 1890.

Facing: Postcard by Raphael Tuck & Sons, printed in Berlin, Germany, circa 1906.

COMPLIMENTS OF THE DOMESTIC S. M. Co.

PRIZE JERSEY BULL PEDRO.

COMPLIMENTS OF THE DOMESTIC S. M. Co.

PRIZE LINCOLN BUCK WILTON

Trade cards,
Domestic Sewing
Machine Co.,
circa 1880.

Travel brochure,
Sitmar Lines,
Italy, 1931, for
Mediterranean
excursions.

Facing:
Luggage label
for Air India,
circa 1955.

Bon Voyage

Travel abroad once was a luxury, whether it was a Mediterranean cruise or a voyage circling the globe. Mementos were prized and carefully preserved as a way to bring back fond memories of good times in distant and exotic lands, from trips by steamship, railway, or airplane. Who can help but smile looking at a travel brochure for a Sitmar Lines 1931 Mediterranean cruise, illustrated with a beaming passenger leaning on the deck? Or chuckle at a 1955 Air-India luggage label for a trip to Paris with a flirtatious man kissing an elegant French woman's hand? Whether it's a parade of safari animals on a 1935 luggage label for the New Stanley Hotel in Nairobi, or a colorful Art Deco travel brochure from the Grand Hotel Pekin, ephemera from adventures abroad give us a glimpse of the Golden Age of travel.

Ferry schedule for Tirrenia Navigation
in German, printed in Italy, 1935.

Cunard White Star Line model of
the *RMS Mauretania*, along with
other Cunard luggage tags.

CUNARD WHITE STAR

QUEEN MARY

TO EUROPE

French Line

Cie Gie

s/s ILE·DE·FRANCE

TRANSATLANTIQUE

STANFORD'S
GENERAL MAP
OF
THE WORLD
ON MERCATOR'S PROJECTION

Equatorial Scale of Nautical Miles
and along respective parallels.

Equator

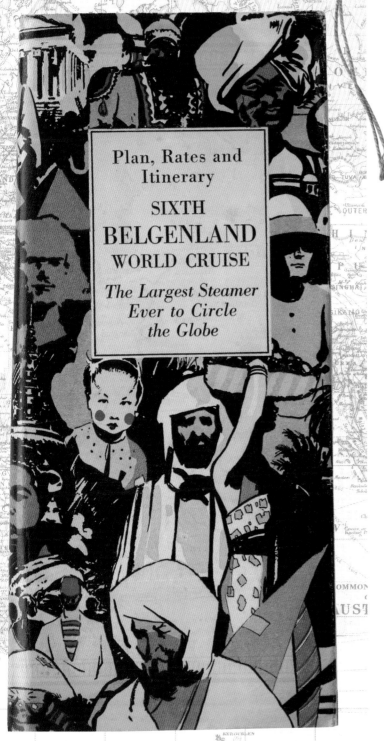

Plan, Rates and Itinerary

SIXTH
BELGENLAND
WORLD CRUISE

*The Largest Steamer
Ever to Circle
the Globe*

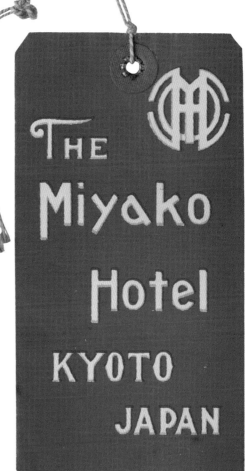

THE Miyako Hotel KYOTO JAPAN

DOMINION LINE.
FIRST CABIN.
WANTED ON VOYAGE
Stateroom   3   Berth
s.s.   Sailing

Facing:
Luggage tag for
Cunard White Star
Line, s/s *Queen
Mary*, 1951.

Luggage label for
the French Line
s/s *Ile de France*,
circa 1954.

This page:
Brochure for world
cruise of 133 days.
Red Star Line, s/s
The Belgenland,
circa 1924.

Luggage tag for
The Miyako Hotel,
Kyoto, Japan, 1930.

Luggage tag for
The Dominion
Line, s/s *New
England*,
circa 1924.

北京 PEKING 北平

GRAND HOTEL
DE PEKIN

PEIPING (PEKING)   CHINA

C. H.

THIS
SEAT IS
Occupied
NORTHWEST
Orient
AIRLINES
PF 38 REV 9-53
PRINTED IN U. S. A.

Peking travel
brochure from
the Grand Hotel
de Pekin, Peking,
China, 1932.

Sepia photo of
couple aboard
steamer,
circa 1921.

Tag for Northwest
Orient Airlines,
1953.

Facing:
Baggage inspec-
tion ticket.
Nassau, Bahamas,
circa 1960.

French Line
Cie Gle TRANSATLANTIQUE

tel que si le
ber en a payé
rant.

LE HAVRE à NEW

ILE DE FRANCE

ebot

(ou tout autre qui lui serā substitué

art du 10 Juillet

OMS ET PRÉNOMS COMPLETS DES PASSAGERS
tels qu'ils figurent sur les passeports

e Celia GOLDSCHER

PAID IN DOLLARS

PARIS - 6, rue Auber
NEW YORK - 610, Fifth Av.   LONDON - 20, Cockspur St.

BILLET DE PASSAGE
PASSAGE TICKET

Passage ticket on French Line, s/s *Ile de France*, issued to Mrs. Celia Goldscher for travel on July 10, 1951.

Facing: Travel brochure for Pan American World Airways, 1961.

Travel guide for American Express, 1928.

Luggage label for Hotel Zeben, The Hague, circa 1958.

SEE EUROPE by PAN AM JET CLIPPER

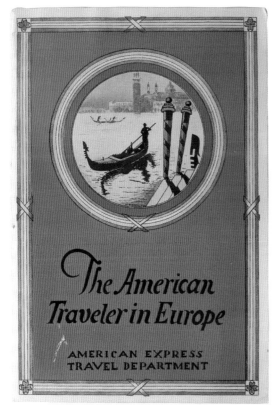

The American Traveler in Europe

AMERICAN EXPRESS
TRAVEL DEPARTMENT

HOTEL
ZEBEN
DEN HAAG
HOLLAND

THE HOTZ HOTELS
CECIL, DELHI. ———— LAURIES, AGRA.

NEW STANLEY HOTEL

Telephone, No. 235.

TO THE
NEW STANLEY

Telegrams, "SNUGGEST."

WE ALL STAY AT THE NEW STANLEY.

NAIROBI, Kenya Colony.

Vintage display
piece of Cavallini &
Co. travel-themed
decorative papers.

Luggage label for
The Hotz Hotels,
India, circa 1940.

Luggage label
for New Stanley
Hotel, Nairobi,
Kenya, 1935.

Assorted
Christmas
wrapping
papers, 1950s.

Facing:
Grouping of boxed
Christmas articles,
various years.

The magic and joy of Christmas appeals to young and old alike. Who can resist Old Saint Nicholas's ruddy cheeks and hearty "Ho, Ho, Ho!" seen on everything from holiday greeting cards, wrapping papers, and labels to sheets of stylish red and green 1936 Christmas Seal stamps? Christmas is magical and transports us to a land of make-believe. If you wrote a letter to the North Pole in 1963, it may have been answered with a jolly "Letter from Santa" by B. F. Goodrich. And did you remember to leave a plate of cookies on the mantel, as an early-twentieth-century storybook from the Hale Brothers Department Store suggests? Christmas tree decorations, from boxes of tinsel icicles to sparking glass balls and even "Doubl-Glo" Mica for under the tree, were saved and cherished each year to rekindle the holiday magic. Collecting Christmas ephemera brings back those happy memories of childhood, when it really did seem possible that Santa Claus would slide down the chimney with presents.

Christmas

Merry Christmas

Santa Claus
Christmas card,
circa 1958.

Facing:
Postcard by
Ellen Clapsaddle,
printed in
Germany, 1907.

Sheet of
Christmas Seals,
American Lung
Association, 1936.

Assorted
Christmas tags,
tapes, and game,
20th century.

Christmas postcard by Ellen Clapsaddle, printed in Germany, 1905.

Christmas gift order form, date unknown.

Christmas envelope, "A Letter from Santa," by B. F. Goodrich, Springfield, MO, 1963.

Facing: Christmas wrapping paper, 1950s.

HERE ARE THE THINGS THAT SANTA CLAUS BRINGS

BUT WHAT BRINGS, SANTA CLAUS?

HALE BROTHERS

First and San Carlos   San Jose

Christmas Story book for Hale Brothers, San Jose, CA, 1931.

Facing:
Box of Doubl-Glo Mica Snow, 1950s.

Christmas postcard, by Ellen Clapsaddle, printed in Germany, 1907.

Christmas postcard, artist unknown, printed in Germany, 1910.

Stack of Ellen Clapsaddle Christmas postcards, circa 1908.

Christmas tag, circa 1921.

"Do not open 'til Christmas" label, 1950s.

Santa Claus die-cut, circa 1960.

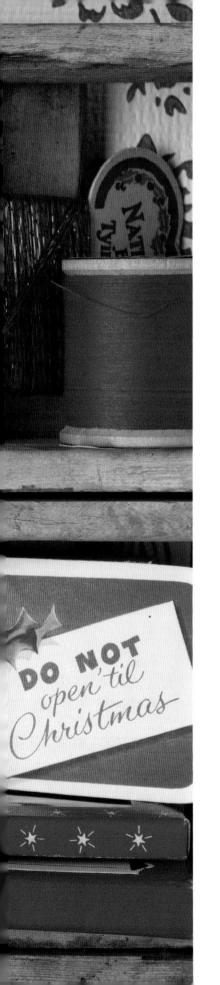

Vintage Christmas articles
housed at Cavallini & Co.

Reflecto-Lite Tree
Top box, by Paper
Novelty Manufacturing
Company, NY, 1938.

Christmas card, circa 1955.

Christmas Seals©, Booth
Envelope, American
Lung Association, 1947.

Cabinet of
curiosities housed
at Cavallini & Co.

Facing:
Hand-colored
plate from
Unterhaltungen
aus der
Naturgeschichte,
by G. T.
Wilhelm, 1813.

Beginning in the Middle Ages, curiosities—objects that spark the imagination and fascinate the mind—were collected and gathered together, often in cabinets, as precursors to our modern museums. Carefully ordered, cataloged, and displayed, curiosities were considered a measure of one's scientific thought and reasoning. Collecting ephemera of curiosities today shows an inquiring mind, whether it is an 1813 hand-colored plate detailing the intricacy of seashells, or a simple illustration of turtles. Starfish and sea urchins swirling across a page; rows of beetles methodically displayed; porcupines, anteaters, armadillos and sloths all drawn in life-like detail—every aspect of the natural world was an object of interest and study.

Curiosities

The greatest mystery of them all was the human body, portrayed in everything from detailed, larger-than-life anatomical charts, to a 1929 illustrated "Portfolio of Anatomical Manikins," to late-nineteenth-century phrenological personality maps of the human head. Our fascination with the curiosities of nature has never waned.

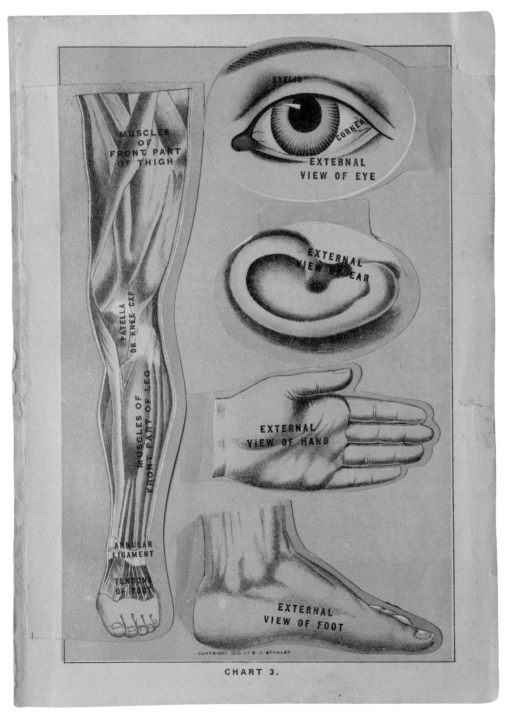

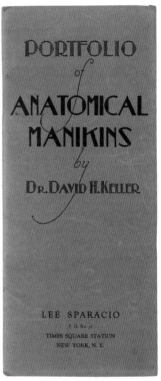

Anatomical bookplate, 1916.

Portfolio of Anatomical Manikins,
by Dr. David H. Keller, NY, 1929.

Facing:
Various anatomical charts, 20th century.

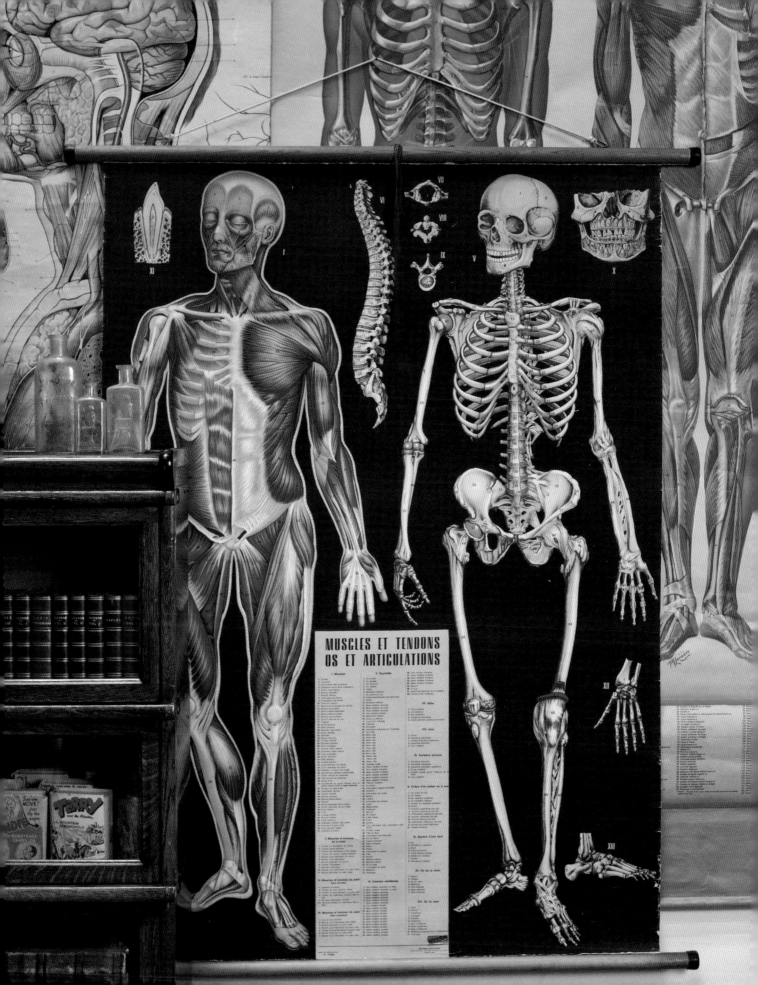

MUSCLES ET TENDONS
OS ET ARTICULATIONS

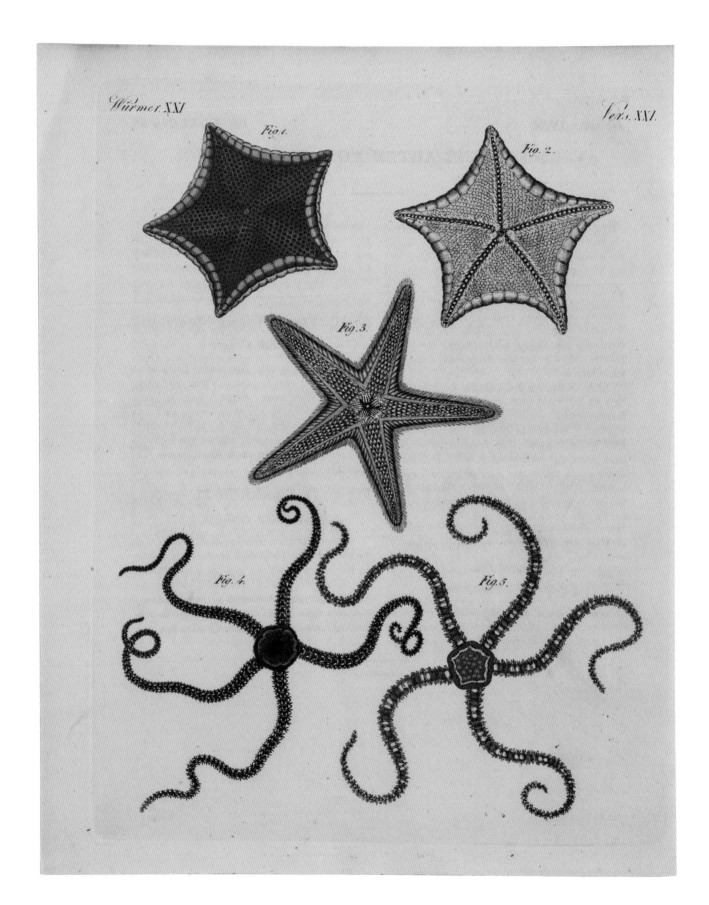

Facing:
Hand-colored
plate, by F. J.
Bertuch, from
*Bilderbuch für
Kinder*, 1805.

This page:
Cabinet of
curiosities housed
at Cavallini & Co.

Various items,
including
hand-colored
bookplates by G. T.
Wilhelm, from the
*Unterhaltungen
aus der
Naturgeschichte*,
1810–13.

Facing:
Anatomical
bookplate, 1916.

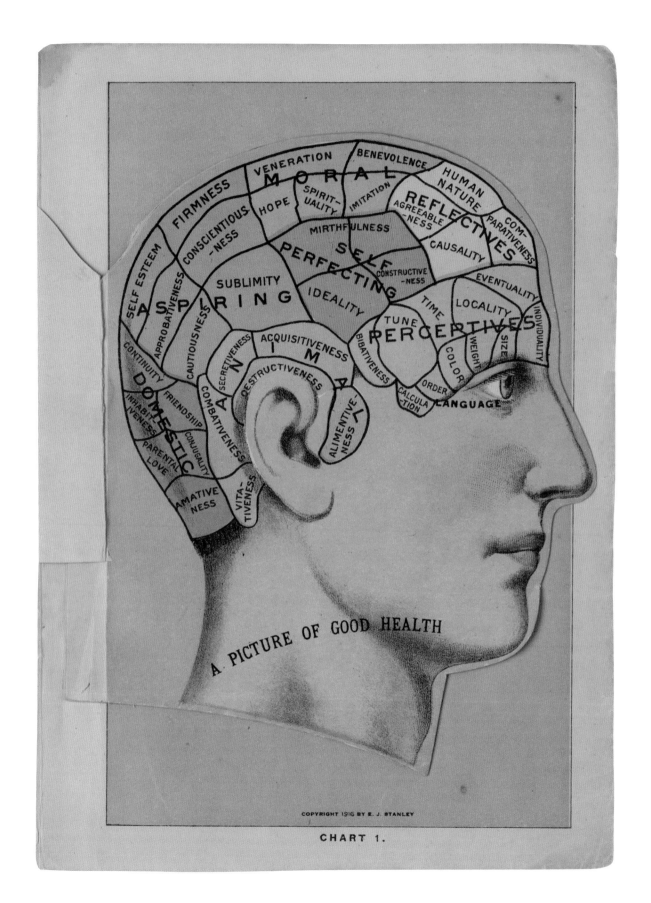

A PICTURE OF GOOD HEALTH

CHART 1.

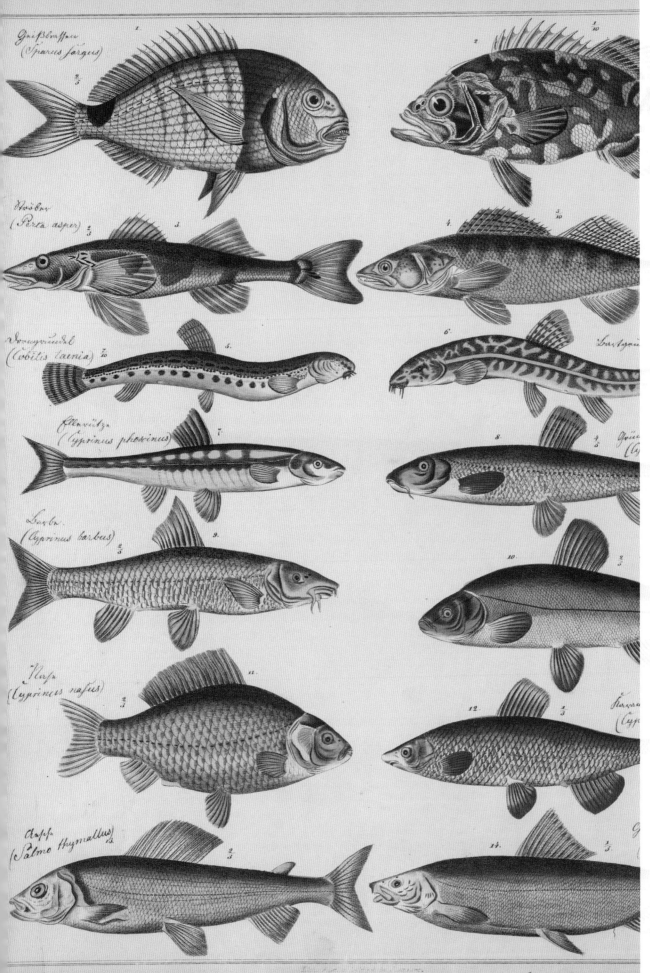

Hand-colored plate by L. Oken, from *Allgemeine Naturgeschichte für alle Stände*, Stuttgart, Germany, 1843.

Facing: Hand-colored plate by G. T. Wilhelm, from *Unterhaltungen aus der Naturgeschichte*, 1813.

Hand-colored plate by F. J. Bertuch, from *Bilderbuch für Kinder*, 1805.

Hand-colored plate, 1845.

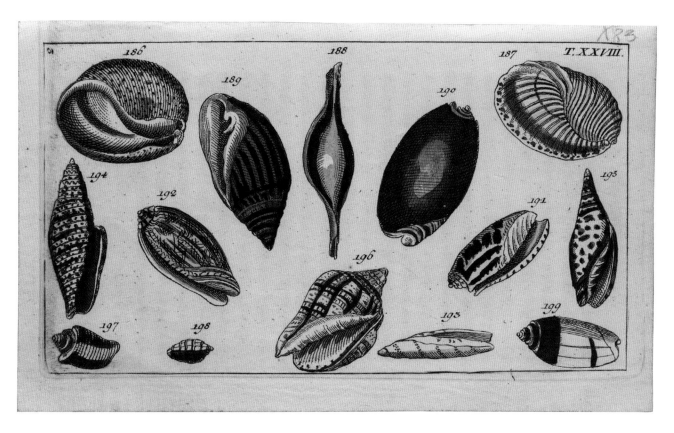

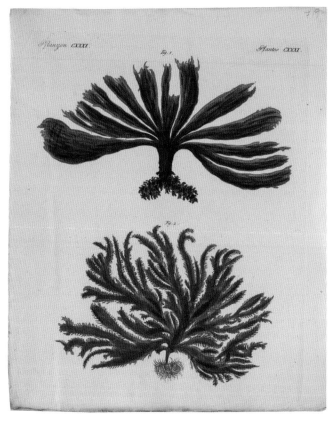

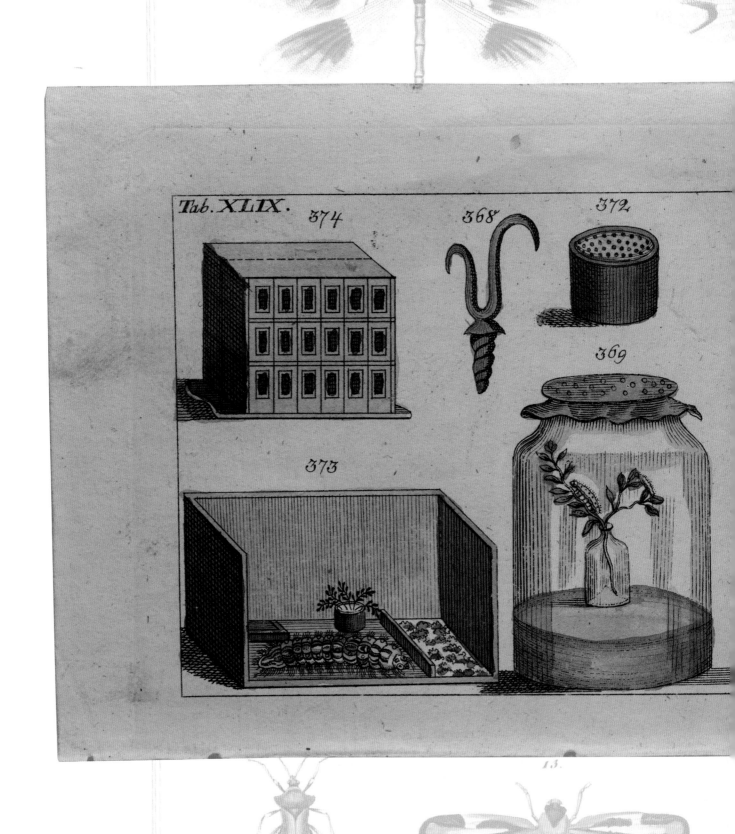

Hand-colored
plate by G. T.
Wilhelm, from
*Unterhaltungen
aus der
Naturgeschichte*,
1810.

Hand-colored
plate by G. T.
Wilhelm, from
*Unterhaltungen
aus der
Naturgeschichte*,
1813.

Robinia Pseudacacia
falsch. Akazie
Angiospermae
Dicotyledonae
Choripetalae
Leguminosae
u. Papilionaceae
(L M)

Facing:
Herbarium species
from herbarium
album, Müllrose,
Germany, 1919.

This page:
Various objects
and hand-colored
plates housed at
Cavallini & Co.

CRIMSON-FLOWERE
PEONY.

Various hand-
colored botanical
imagery, England.

Facing:
Bird trade card for
T. J. Wing, Agent,
by American Cigar
Co., Westfield,
MA, 1882.

Flora and Fauna

Whether it is delicate hand-colored plates from a nineteenth-century botanical book, or a handsome chromolithographed bookplate from an 1890 volume of *British Birds and Their Eggs*, images of flora and fauna have a timeless and classic appeal. The graceful beauty of birds was a popular subject for trade cards, such as a multihued peacock on an 1890 French trade card, or the delicate swoop of a sparrow captured for a White Sewing Machine trade card of the same period.

Iridescent butterflies evoked nature's ephemeral beauty, and avid collectors delicately pinned and displayed them in glass cases. Plant life was assiduously studied and collected as well, from the mushrooms depicted in a hand-colored plate of an 1805 volume, to the detailed fronds of ferns depicted in a bookplate from the 1869 book *Grasses, Sedges, and Ferns of Great Britain*. Images of plant and animal life, meticulously rendered in fine detail, bring to life the wonders of the natural world.

Bound copy of
*The Floricultural
Cabinet and
Florists'
Magazine*, London,
England, 1850.

Facing:
Bookplate from
*Allgemeine
Naturgeschichte
für alle Ständ*, by
L. Oken. Stuttgart,
Germany, 1843.

FLORICULTURAL C

APRIL, 18

ILLUSTRATIO

GEANT DES BATAILLES.—HYBRID

" Just like love is this fine R
Heavenly fragrance round
Yet tears its dewy leaves d
And in the midst of briars
Just like love.

" Called to bloom upon the
Since rough thorns the ste
They must be gather'd wit
And with it to the heart b
Just like love."

THE Rose is pre-eminently the FLOWE
very perfection of floral realities, and
QUEEN OF FLOWERS. It is considered
Beauty. Berkeley, in his Utopia, descri
passion by presenting to the fair beloved a
open: if the lady accepted and wore the
favour his pretensions. As time increa
followed up the first present by that of a
succeeded by one full-blown; and if the
considered as engaged for life.

Poetry is lavish of Roses; it heaps the
crowns, twines them into arbours, forges
them the goblet used in festivals, and
beauty: nay, not only delights to bring
occasion, but seizes each particular beau
comparison with the loveliest works of n
as sweet as a Rose; rosy-clouds; rosy-che
rosy-dawns, &c.

VOL. XVIII. No. 40.—*N.S.*

Jay.

Chough.

Magpie.

Alpine Chough.

Hooded Crow.

Nutcracker.

Raven.

Jackdaw.

Raven.

Carrion Crow.

Rook.

Carrion Crow.

Pawson & Brailsford Lith Sheffield

Left:
Various flora and fauna bookplates housed at Cavallini & Co.

Chromolithograph bookplate from *History of British Birds and their Eggs*, by Pawson & Brailsford Lith, Sheffield, UK, circa 1890.

A Parroqueet from Angola.   Eleazar Albin Del July 30. 1735.

THE WHITE IS KING
One Million Now in Use.

Facing:
Hand-colored plate
from *A Natural
History of Birds*,
by Eleazar Albin.
London, UK, 1735.

This page:
Peacock trade
card, French,
circa 1890.

Bird trade card
for White Sewing
Machine Company,
circa 1890.

Hand-colored
bookplate from
*Unterhaltungen
aus der
Naturgeschicht*,
by G. T.
Wilhelm, 1813.

Facing:
Herbarium species
from Winslow,
ME, 1903.

PALE MOUNTAIN POLYPODY,
Polypodium phegopteris.

Facing:
Various
19th-century
envelopes and
trade cards.

Chromolithograph
bookplate from
*The Grasses,
Sedges, and
Ferns of Great
Britain,* by Anne
Pratt, London,
England, 1869.

Facing:
Hand-colored plate
from *Bilderbuch
für Kinder*, by
F. J. Bertuch, 1805.

Shadow box of
butterflies from
Deyrolle, Paris,
France, early 20th
century, along with
various 19th- and
20th-century
trade cards and
bookplates.

Vignette of printing blocks, rubber stamps, and other alphabetic scholastic charts.

Facing: Registered letter cover postmarked July 28, 1916, from South Tottenham to Enfield, England.

ritten ephemera transports us back to a time when people expressed themselves elegantly with pen and paper, when writing was an art, each letter of the alphabet carefully drawn and illustrated. Instruction in the art of writing began in school with charts and diagrams of each letter form.

In those days, mail delivery was anticipated with pleasure and excitement. Envelopes were adorned with colorful stamps and perhaps even an elegant wax seal, such as a registered English letter postmarked July 28, 1916, shows. "First Day," "First Flight," and souvenir covers were sent empty and mailed simply to commemorate an occasion. Documents such as an elegantly scripted Italian birth certificate dated July 18, 1813, carefully preserved for over two hundred years, and an airmailed envelope adorned with fine penmanship provide a glimpse into times long past. They pique our curiosity about the sender and the recipient.

Letters and Correspondence

Cover for FAM-18 First Flight Clipper Airmail, May 20, 1939.

Postcard postmarked from Canterbury to London, England, on December 5, 2000, via Post Office Express.

Facing:
Folded stampless letter dated April 8, 1812, from Paris to Bourges, France.

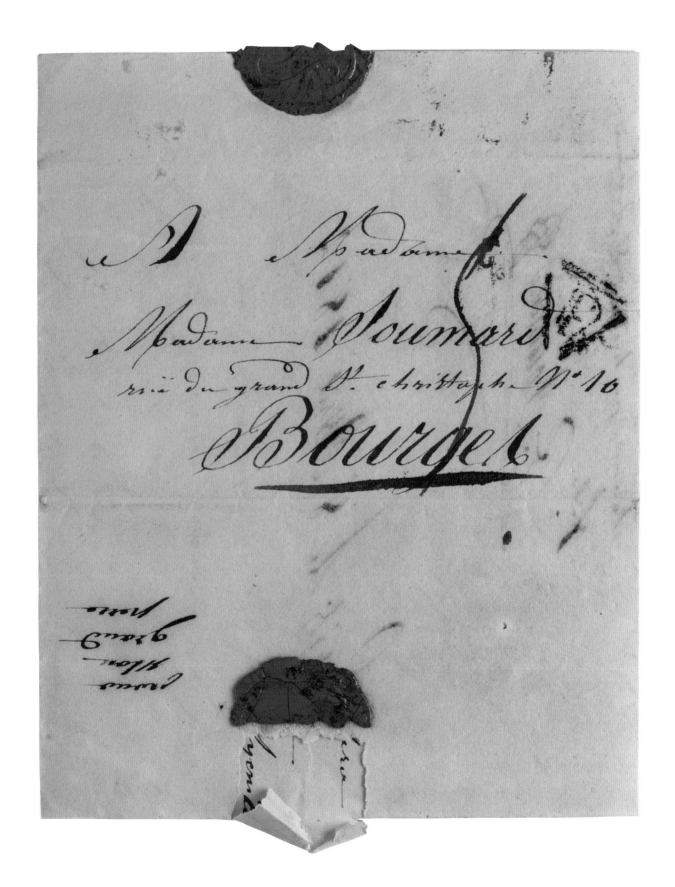

32ᵉ LEÇON

ec el er

ef es ex

balance

ç   ça ço çu cé

Ç   ça ço çu cé

1. gla ce ciel cinq reçu ce

2. pla ce sau ce mer ci mé de c

3. Une belle gla ce

4. Le bon ma çon

5. La gran de pla ce

6. La fa ça de de l'é co le

7. La cein tu

8. Cé ci le a u n

9. Yvet te a vu la

10. Le gar

11. Le ma çon a u

12. Le gar çon du ma çon se nom

13. Yvet te a par lé à Lu cien le gar çon du m

MacLEA
of W
By
PR
COMPEND
For Firs

Containing Copies for Study, and
the Pupil's Prog

Part I. Printing (Manuscrip

NAME OF PUPIL ....

SCHOOL ....

W. J. GAGE & CO

Left:
French and English manuals for methods of writing.

This page:
Partial view of a folded passport issued in Florence, Italy, in December 1816, detailing passages in 1817.

ESTRATTO

Da' registri degli atti di Nascita dell' Anno

N.° d'ordine _____ Fol.

L'anno milleottocento *tredici* a *otto* del mese di *Luglio* — ad ore *ventidue* Avanti di noi *ff...* *no Casovita Elletto* _____ ed Uffiziale dello Stato Civile del Comune di *Giuggano* Provincia di Napoli, è comparso *il Syn Gaetano Peffoli di anni quarantacinque*

di professione *Legale*
domiciliato *Barba Giffema dell'alto 1822*
ed a dichiarato *che il 8 più delpad mep a don di ni è nato nella sua propria casa dale dichiarante, dalla Signora Maria Santeria, sua moglie legittima, e unni trenta sei, una bambina che si trap vota*

cui si è dato il nome di *Maria, Angela, Elisabetta, erozia, frene, Ffofa, Vertofa, Adelaide, Juan, Gaetana, Antonia, Luigia*

La presentazione, e dichiarazione si è fatta alla presenza di *Luigi Scala Ffade Miniola*
di anni *quarantasette* di professione *funessedente*
domiciliato *Frada S. Biagio dei dibrai 1821*
e di *Arhezzo Tarantino* di anni *quaranta*
di professione *Legale* —
domiciliato *il R le Ferra dell'Aliota 1822*

Facing:
Italian birth certificate from July 18, 1813.

This page: Registered letter cover postmarked May 12, 1922, from Threadneedles to Prestbury, Gloucestershire, England.

First flight cover postmarked April 1, 1930, from Charlotte, NC, to Detroit, MI.

First flight cover postmarked March 1, 1929, from Daytona Beach, FL, to New York City.

Left:
Various 19th- and
20th-century
folded stamped
letters, France.

This page:
Folded stampless
letter postmarked
September 24,
1844 from Crest to
Colmar, France.

Folded business
document
addressed
to Bordeaux,
France, 1783.

Facing:
Various stamped
letters, business
and personal,
20th century.

This page:
Registered letter
cover postmarked
July 4, 1921,
from Bohicon,
Dahomey, to Nyon,
Switzerland.

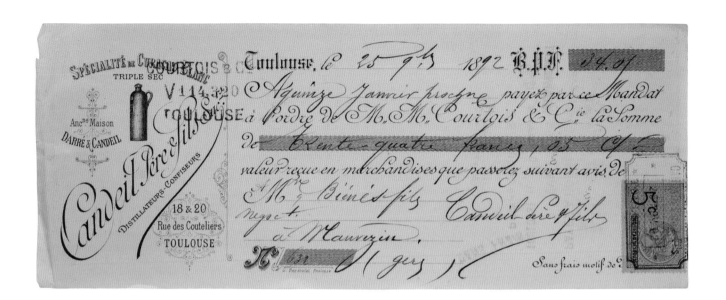

Business check
issued in Toulouse,
France, on
September 25,
1892.

Hand-illustrated
cover postmarked
April 4, 1927,
from Ponca City,
OK, to Morton

Salt Company,
Hutchinson, KS.

Facing:
Souvenir cover
of Coronation of
Queen Elizabeth
II, postmarked on
May 25, 1953,
to and from

Auckland, New
Zealand.

Letter cover
postmarked from
Marseille, France,
on November 11,
1926.

Hamilton
Manufacturing
printer's
cabinet housing
various maps at
Cavallini & Co.

Facing:
Map of Tokyo
and Surrounding
Districts,
March 1953.

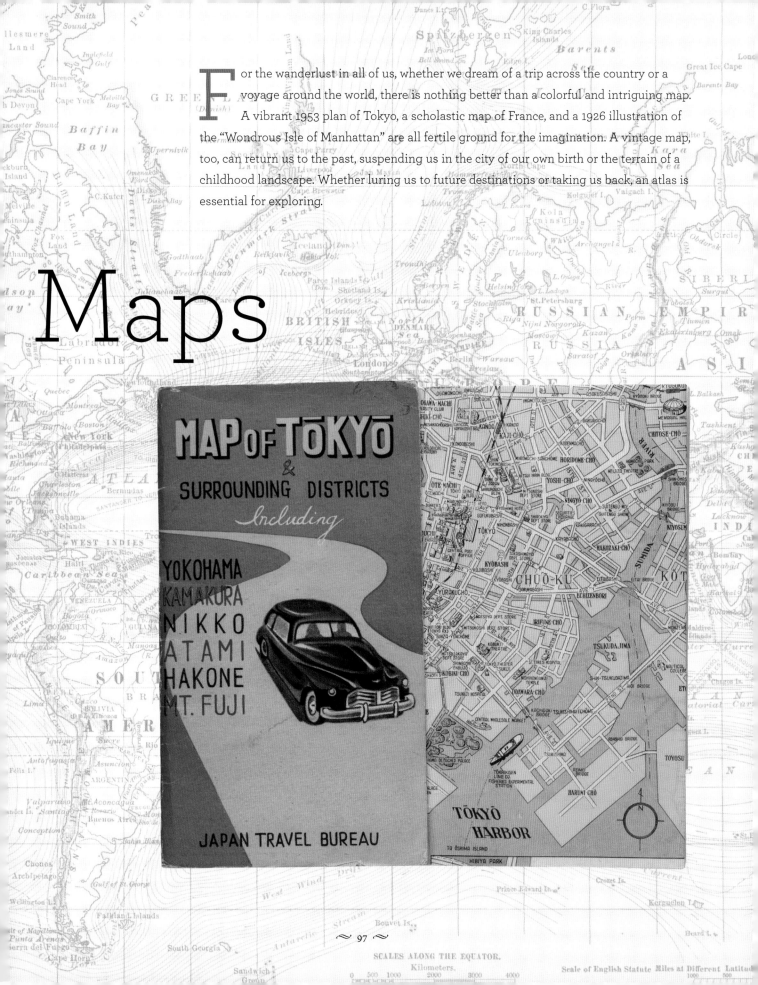

For the wanderlust in all of us, whether we dream of a trip across the country or a voyage around the world, there is nothing better than a colorful and intriguing map. A vibrant 1953 plan of Tokyo, a scholastic map of France, and a 1926 illustration of the "Wondrous Isle of Manhattan" are all fertile ground for the imagination. A vintage map, too, can return us to the past, suspending us in the city of our own birth or the terrain of a childhood landscape. Whether luring us to future destinations or taking us back, an atlas is essential for exploring.

Maps

MAP OF TOKYO
& SURROUNDING DISTRICTS
Including

YOKOHAMA
KAMAKURA
NIKKO
ATAMI
HAKONE
MT. FUJI

JAPAN TRAVEL BUREAU

TŌKYŌ HARBOR

Hand-colored
map of Italy,
date unknown.

Facing:
Scholastic political
map of France,
circa 1921.

ANGLETERRE

MER DU NORD

Bruxelles

BELGIQUE

ALLEMAGNE

LA MANCHE

LUXEMBOURG

le Havre

Rouen

Reims

Metz

Sarrebr

Nancy

Strasbour

PARIS

Versailles

Chartres

Orléans

Troyes

Chaumont

Épinal

Colmar

Rennes

le Mans

Auxerre

Dijon

Besançon

Belfort

Nantes

Tours

Blois

Bourges

Nevers

Berne

SUISSE

Poitiers

Châteauroux

Moulins

Mâcon

Bourg

la Roche-s-Yon

Niort

Guéret

Lyon

Annecy

La Rochelle

Limoges

Clermont-Fd

St-Étienne

Chambéry

Angoulême

Tulle

le Puy

Valence

Grenoble

Périgueux

Aurillac

Privas

Gap

Bordeaux

Mende

Digne

Cahors

Rodez

Nice

Agen

Montauban

Albi

Nîmes

Avignon

Mont-de-Marsan

Auch

Montpellier

Draguignan

Toulouse

Marseille

Pau

Tarbes

Carcassonne

Toulon

Foix

MER MÉDITERRANÉE

Perpignan

ESPAGNE

ANDORRE

CARTE N.º 12

FRANCE POLITIQUE

Départements
Densité de la Population
Grandes Villes
Anciennes Provinces

Échelle de 1: 1.000.000 (Soit 1cm pour 10 Kil.)

ANCIENNES PROVINCES

VILLES

DENSITÉ DE LA POPULATION

CORSE

Ajaccio

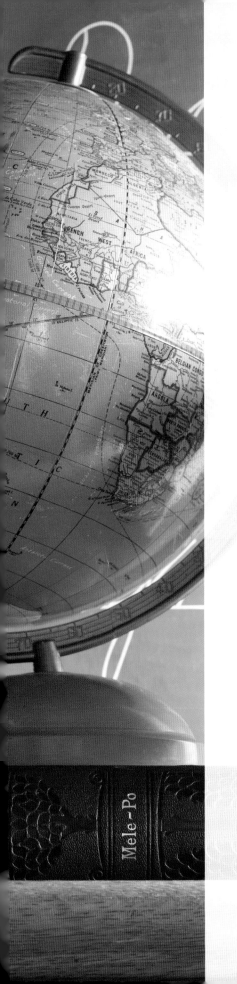

Various paper
and metal globes,
20th century.

Die-cut folding
trade card to
combat malaria,
for Esanofele,
Italy, 1920.

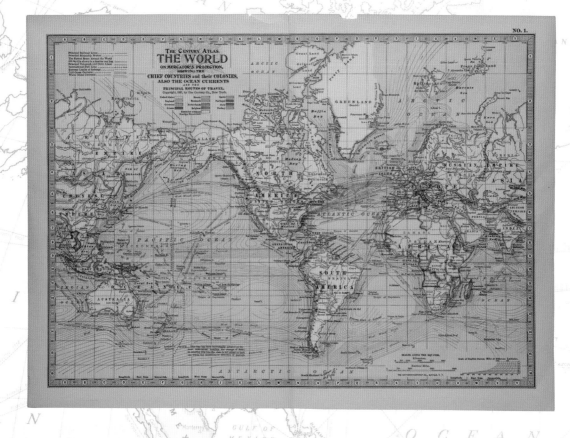

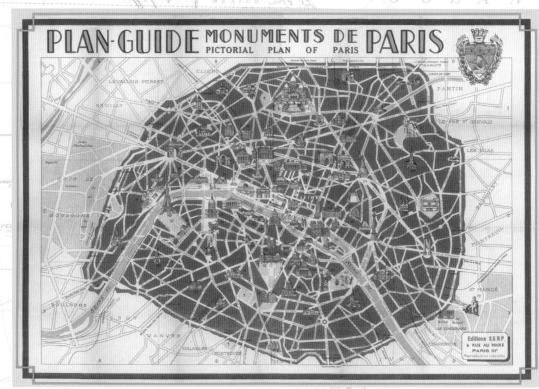

COLLECTION
DES
CARTES TARIDE

GRANDE CARTE
DE L'

EUROPE
CENTRALE

NOUVELLES FRONTIÈRES

Prix : **3** francs.

Sur toile pliée: 13 francs. — Sur toile avec baguettes: 28 francs.

CARTES TARIDE

18-20, Boulevard Saint-Denis, PARIS (X⁰).

Deutsche Städte-Ausstellung
DRESDEN
1903

Weltausstellung
BRÜSSEL
1910

Silberne Medaille

PHARUS-
PLAN
BERLIN

MIT VORORTEN

Eingetragene Schutzmarke

Fahrtfinder-Ausgabe

Pharus Verlag G.m.b.H.
Berlin SW 68
Linden-Strasse 3.

Mittel Ausgabe

Facing:
Map of the World,
*The Century
Atlas,* 1897.

Pictorial map
of Paris and its
monuments,
date unknown.

This page:
Cover to folded
map of Central
Europe, 1924.

Cover to folded
Berlin map by
Pharus, 1914.

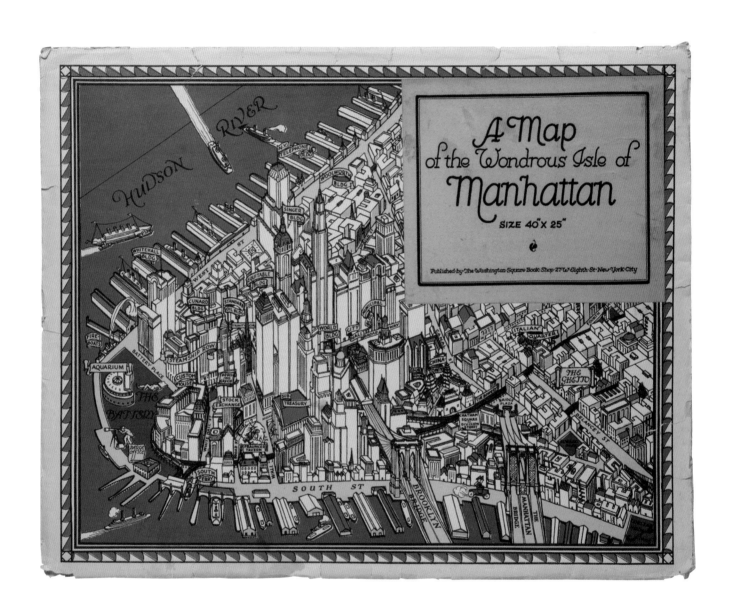

Protective sleeve
for A Map of the
Wondrous Isle of
Manhattan, 1926.

Facing:
Schoolroom
political map of
the British Isles, by
Philips', circa 1930.

PHILIPS'
SCHOOL-ROOM MAP
OF THE
RITISH ISLES
POLITICAL
Scale 1:750,000 (11·8 m. = 1 inch)
STATUTE MILES

EXPLANATION

Collection of various map-related products and original maps.

Assemblage of
Italian guidebooks
and maps with
Italian opera
librettos.

Maps of Rome
and Florence
with 18th-century
document.

Acollection of colorful vintage guidebooks of Pisa, Venice, and Rome; a stack of Italian opera librettos; a bright red 1905 luggage tag from the Palace Hotel in Milan; or a 1927 postcard of winding roads hugging the Amalfi Coast: Italian souvenirs suggest the richness of Italy. A Pan American World Airways brochure from 1954 with a couple gliding serenely in a gondola along the Grand Canal in Venice evokes the romance of Italy.

Italy

A postcard of the Colosseum sent in 1923 or a 1908 souvenir postcard album from Florence, with its fragile tissue paper still intact, steps us back in time. Mementos from Italy return us to the warmth and artistry of its culture.

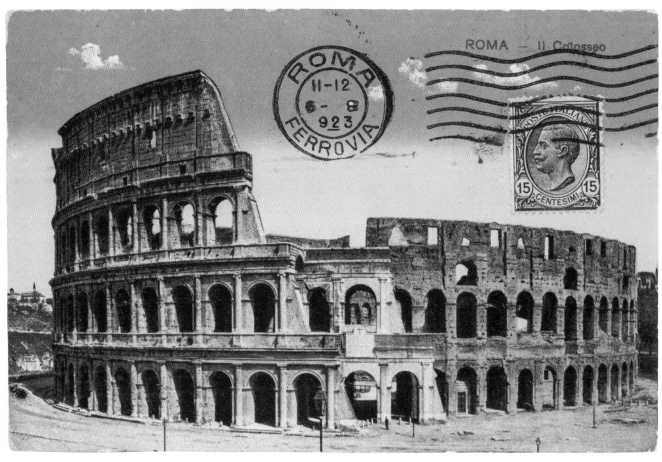

Facing:
Luggage label from Palace Hotel, Milan, 1905.

Postcard of Italian Lakes by ENIT (the Italian government tourist board), postmarked on April 29, 1937, from Rome to Torino, Italy.

Postcard of the Colosseum, Rome, postmarked December 11, 1923, from Rome to Viareggio, Italy.

This page: Various Italian Line items, including silver water pot.

Postcard of Amalfi
by ENIT, 1927.

Rome and Environs
guidebook, 1924.

ROME
AND
ENVIRONS

A. SCROCCHI - EDITOR
MILAN - ROME

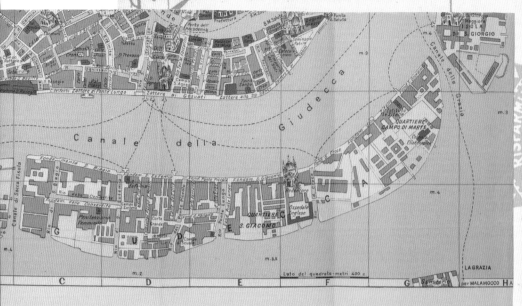

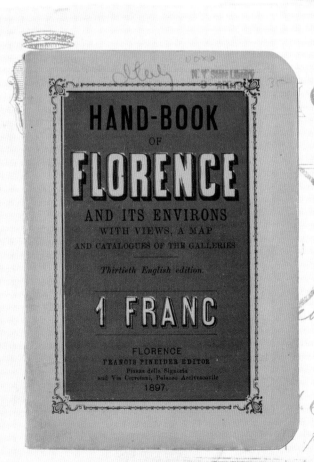

Facing:
Guidebook and
map of Venice,
date unknown.

*Hand-Book of
Florence and Its
Enviorns*, 1897.

Luggage label for
Trovatore Hotel,
San Marco, Venice,
circa 1955.

This page:
Italy and
Rome travel
brochure by Pan
American World
Airways, 1954.

ITALY
and ROME

PAN AMERICAN WORLD AIRWAYS
System of the Flying Clippers

Postcard of Assisi by
ENIT, postmarked
in 1932 from Assisi
to Foggia, Italy.

Artistic views of
Venice, circa 1900.

Italian brochures by
ENIT, circa 1930.

Firenze - La Facciata della Cattedrale
(Architetto De Fabris)

PISA - Il Campanile della Cattedrale   1079

Facing:
Various early-
20th-century
Italian postcards
and a scholastic
map of Italy.

This page:
Souvenir
postcard album of
Florence, 1908.

Postcard of Pisa,
postmarked in
1895 from Pisa to
New Orleans, LA.

Facing:
Guidebook of Pisa
by ENIT, 1934.

This page:
Postcard of
Palermo, Sicily,
by ENIT, 1925.

Luggage label
from Gallia
Excelsior Hotel,
Milan, circa 1950.

Postcard of
Taormina, Sicily,
by ENIT, 1927.

Various items from
the Coronation of
Queen Elizabeth
II, 1953.

Facing:
Luggage label
for Savoy Hotel,
London, circa 1930.

Civilized and proper tradition is the backbone of the English way of life. Attending the coronation of the queen would have been the highlight of any trip to London, and pamphlets, postcards, and even matchbooks carefully preserved memories of the occasion: a postcard of Her Majesty Queen Elizabeth II, postmarked December 5, 1952, captures the iconic figure in her youth.

In its day, Trans World Airways was the finest way to fly. Lucky passengers received a handy booklet of travel tips for Britain in 1960. Luggage labels and receipts would have been from the very best hotels—the Regent Palace, Royal Court, Savoy, and Cumberland.

To navigate the streets of London, guidebooks and maps were a must, from a 1948 London trams and trolleys pamphlet to a collection of colorful maps of central London. And no trip to London would be complete without watching the changing of the guard at Buckingham Palace, as a 1955 children's map of London reminds us.

London

Her Majesty Queen Elizabeth II

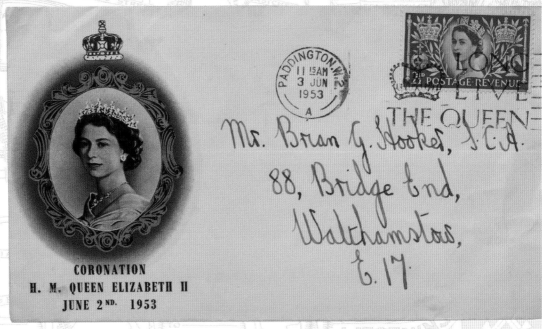

Facing:
Tuck's Coronation
postcard of Her Majesty
Queen Elizabeth II,
postmarked
December 5, 1952.

This page:
Coronation Scrap
Book, 1953.
Coronation cover,
postmarked June 3,
1953, from Paddington
to Walthamstow,
London, England.

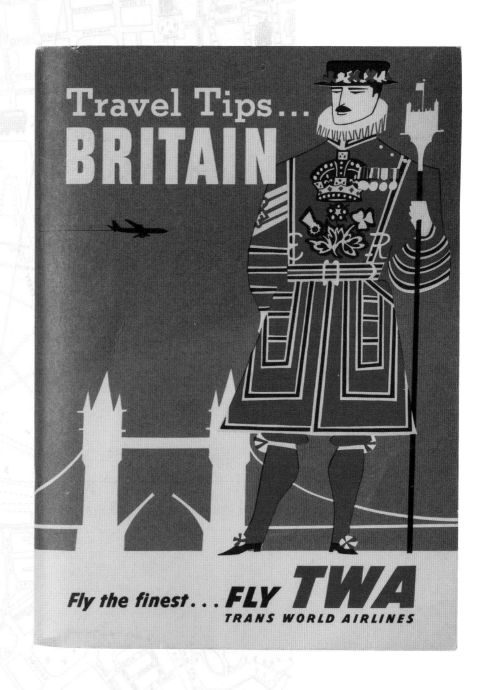

London imagery
includes map
and guide, 20th
century.

Travel guide
of Britain for
Trans World
Airlines, 1960.

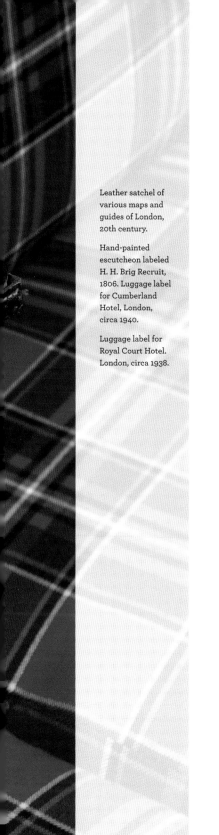

Leather satchel of various maps and guides of London, 20th century.

Hand-painted escutcheon labeled H. H. Brig Recruit, 1806. Luggage label for Cumberland Hotel, London, circa 1940.

Luggage label for Royal Court Hotel. London, circa 1938.

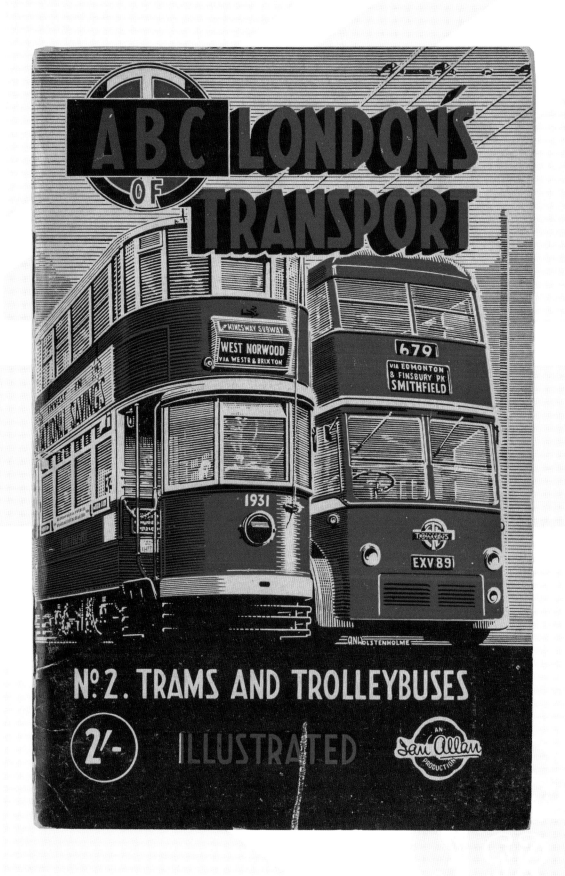

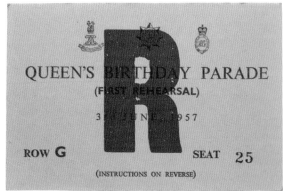

Collection
of London
correspondence
ranging from
1846 to 1937.

Ticket for Queen's
Birthday Parade
rehearsal, London,
June 3, 1957.

Picture souvenir
book of London,
by Valentine &
Sons Ltd., London,
circa 1947.

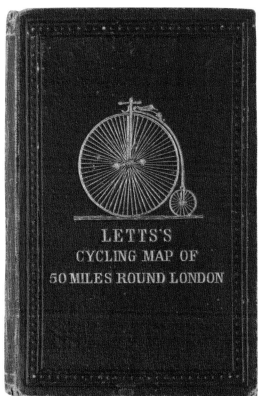

LETTS'S
CYCLING MAP OF
50 MILES ROUND LONDON

Letts's Cycling Map of 50 Miles Round London, 1884.

The ABC Guide to London for E. J. Larby, Ltd., London, 1916.

Picture Map of London by Chichester's, circa 1950.

Assorted London letters and correspondence, 20th century.

Facing: Matchbook for the Coronation of Queen Elizabeth II, 1953.

Postcard for the Coronation of Queen Elizabeth II, 1953.

Her Majesty's Coronation 1953

Elizabeth R 1953

CLOSE COVER BEFORE STRIKING MATCH

Her Majesty Queen Elizabeth II

Barrister cabinet of various Paris-related ephemera, including maps, guides, and brochures, late 18th to mid-20th century.

Facing: Newspaper *Le Petit Parisien*, December 21, 1935.

From the iconic Eiffel Tower and the Champs-Elysees to the majestic Arc de
Triumphe and Trocadero, Paris is one of the most beloved cities in the world.
A bundle of *Le Petite Parisien* newspapers from 1935, an ordinary 1908 business
check adorned with multihued stamps, even a 1939 French National Lottery ticket—all
depict life in Paris from a different time.

Paris

Paris has always been and remains the sophisticated capital of culture and fine cuisine.
A box of fine Lombart French chocolates, souvenir maps, guidebooks, brochures, postcards,
and a stereoscopic view of the Paris Exposition of 1900 are mementos recalling the
romance of the City of Light.

A LA VILLE DE St DENIS

Le moyen de descendre commodément sans faire queue aux ascenseurs ou aux escaliers.

Imp. H.Sicard, Paris

11725—Trocadero Entrance to the Exposition—Colonial Section in Foreground, Paris, 1900.

Facing:
Trade card for a la Ville de Saint-Denis department store, Paris, France, circa 1900.

This page:
Chromolithograph label Vue de Paris, circa 1900.

Stereoscopic view card of the Trocadero and Eiffel Tower for the Paris Exposition, 1900.

Business check
issued by
Charles Golay Fils,
Paris, France, on
December 1,
1908.

Official ticket
issued by the
French National
Lottery, April 1939.

Facing:
Array of
20th-century
Parisian ephemera.

38. — PARIS. — Le Moulin Rouge

Paris 20 mars 1906

Appareils d'observations scientifiques.

300 m. du sol.

Le Phare.

Attache des Antennes de la Télégraphie sans fil.

3375   PARIS. — Le Sommet de la Tour Eiffel.

3'50

Paris

E. BRIAN, 23, Rue d'Arcole, Paris

24 Vues Détachables

LL

Facing:
Printed Cavallini & Co. Paris decorative paper, along with original 20th-century Parisian ephemera.

This page:
Postcard of the Moulin Rouge, Paris, France, postmarked March 21, 1906.

Postcard of the summit of the Eiffel Tower, postmarked 1897.

Souvenir postcard book of views of Paris, circa 1920.

Folded letter
postmarked from
New York to Paris
on September
5, 1866.

Reverse envelope
cover with wax
seals, postmarked
February 8,
1893, to Hotel
St. George,
Paris, France.

Facing:
Typographic
specimen from
Album de Lettres.
Paris, France, 1901.

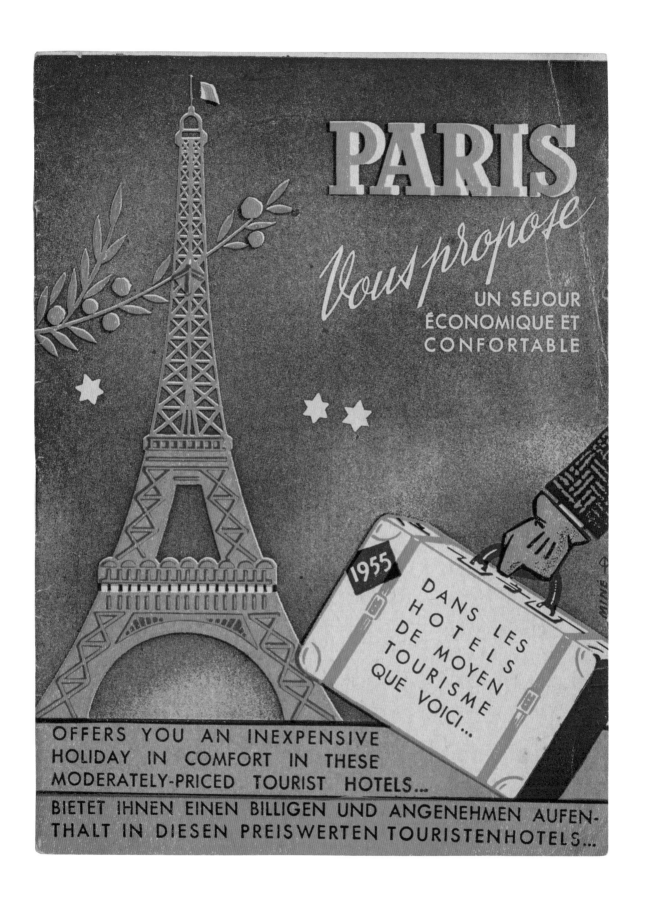

CARTE POSTALE

ceptant pas la correspondance au recto, se renseigner à la Po...

ADRESSE

Facing:
Brochure for
Parisian tourist
hotels, 1955.

This page:
Cabinet at
Cavallini & Co.
housing early
20th-century
Parisian postcards.

Various late-19th and early-20th-century French chocolate labels and packaging.

Facing: French billhead correspondence, January 18, 1912.

Air France map of Paris, 1955.

Postcard of Trocadero of Paris postmarked from Paris to New Haven, CT, on August 3, 1905.

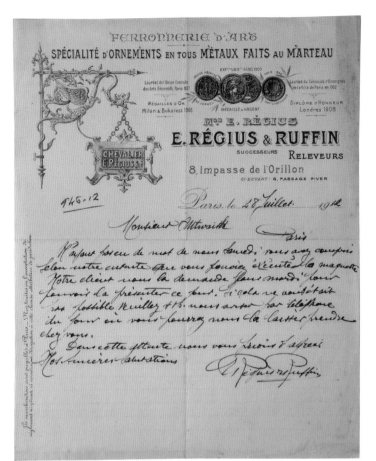

Collection of
20th-century
New York City–
themed ephemera,
including souvenir
decals, maps,
postcard folders,
and first-day cover.

Facing:
Tourist booklet
*New York the
Wonder City*, 1937.

Tourist booklet
*Picture Book of
New York*, 1947.

New York is one of the largest cities in the world, and every visitor would have had a guidebook, from an early 1912 booklet for the "Wonder City" (New York's nickname in the days before "The Big Apple") to a colorful 1947 *Picture Book of New York* adorned with the Statue of Liberty. The bright lights of Times Square, the graceful arches of the Brooklyn Bridge, and streetscapes of towering skyscrapers were all proudly displayed in period maps and brochures.

The majestic skyline is seen best from the top of the Empire State Building, (the tallest manmade building in the world), as a souvenir pennant proclaims, or one could remember his or her trip in the 1950s with a windshield decal for their car. Ephemera of every type, from maps and brochures to postcards and trade cards, would have been collected and perhaps displayed in a tourist's New York postcard album from the early twentieth century.

New York

Observatory
**EMPIRE
STATE**
BUILDING

OPEN 7 DAYS
A WEEK
9:30 a.m.
to MIDNIGHT

NEW YORK
CITY MAP

The
KNOTT
HOTELS
NEW YORK
★

Facing:
Tourist brochure
of Empire
State Building
Observatory,
circa 1950.

Map of New
York City by The
Knott Hotels,
New York, 1935.

This page:
Tourist booklet
*New York: The
Wonder City*, 1945.

COPYRIGHT 1939 BY CURT TEICH & CO., INC., CHICAGO, U.S.

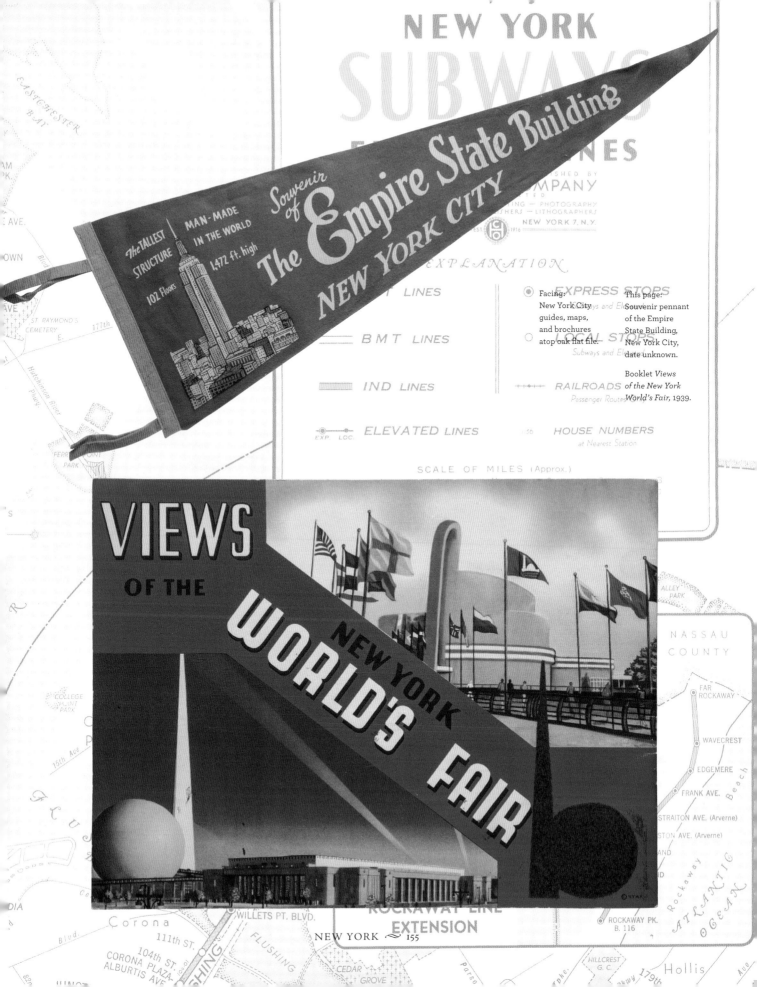

NEW YORK
SUBWAYS
LINES
...NES

PUBLISHED BY
...COMPANY
...TED
...ING — PHOTOGRAPHY
...HERS — LITHOGRAPHERS
NEW YORK 7, N.Y.

EXPLANATION

...T LINES

BMT LINES

IND LINES

ELEVATED LINES
EXP. LOC.

Facing:
New York City
guides, maps,
and brochures
atop oak flat file.

EXPRESS STOPS
...ys and Ele...

LOCAL STOPS
Subways and El...

RAILROADS
Passenger Routes

HOUSE NUMBERS
at Nearest Station

This page:
Souvenir pennant
of the Empire
State Building,
New York City,
date unknown.

Booklet *Views
of the New York
World's Fair*, 1939.

SCALE OF MILES (Approx.)

Souvenir of
The Empire State Building
NEW YORK CITY

The TALLEST
STRUCTURE
MAN-MADE
IN THE WORLD
1,472 ft. high
102 Floors

VIEWS
OF THE
NEW YORK
WORLD'S
FAIR

Tourist booklet
*New York City:
Metropolis of the
World,* circa 1935.

Tourist guide *New
York: The Golden
Guide of the
Metropolis,* 1939.

Windshield decal
Empire State
Building, New
York, 1950s.

Facing:
New York postcard
album filled with
postcards and
trade cards, early
20th century.

Grand Central Terminal Station, New York City.

REETINGS From NEW YORK

Card

PRIVATE MAILING CARD

Miss

Helene Hillman

POST CARD

POST CARD

Statue of Liberty
The Statue of Liberty stands upon Bedloe's Island, 1¾ miles southwest from the Battery. Designed by August Bartholdi. It is 150 feet in height, standing upon a pedestal 155 feet, and symbolizes "Liberty Enlightening the World."

FLAT IRON BUILDING, BROADWAY AND FIFTH AVENUE, NEW YORK CITY. Fuller Building, generally known as the Flat Iron Building, stands at the intersection of Broadway and Fifth Avenue 23rd Street. Was the first steel fra world. It is 300 sq. ft. of floor s sq. ft. under the

PUBLISHED BY THE UNION NEWS COMPANY

THE "NEW SINGER"

ONLY OFFICIALLY AUTHORIZED EDITION

Trade card Liberty Enlightening the World, by Merrick Thread Co., circa 1890.

Facing: Postcard Statue of Liberty, postmarked from New York City to Detroit, MI, on December 29, 1905.

Postcard folder Greetings from New York, circa 1955.

Street guide to New York and map of Manhattan and The Bronx, 1936.

STATUE OF LIBERTY, NEW YORK

Best Wishes for a Happy and prosperous New Year.

Edw. Mc Namee

1914. ILL. POST-CARD CO., N.Y.

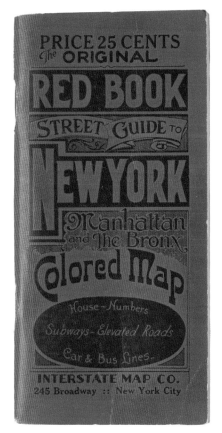

Tourist booklet *New York The Wonder City*, 1912.

Right: Collection of 20th-century New York City–themed ephemera, including souvenir decals, maps, postcard folders, and first-flight cover.

Collection of San
Francisco items,
including Cavallini
& Co.'s published
decorative paper
and postcards.

Facing:
Postcard, Ferry
Building of
San Francisco
postmarked from
San Francisco
to Kennedy,
New York, on
June 2, 1941.

Cable cars clanging up its steep hillsides, rows of colorful Victorian homes lining the streets, and vendors in Chinatown selling their wares all make San Francisco lively, fun, and full of adventure. When souvenirs are revisited, they still make us smile. A 1951 decal brings back fond memories of a stroll on Fisherman's Wharf and the view from Coit Tower.

San Francisco

The Golden Gate Bridge—San Francisco's most famous icon—is displayed on everything from postcards, letters, and stamps to souvenir pieces of redwood from its construction. A 1900s ticket for a dip in Sutro Baths, toy cable cars still in their colorful cardboard boxes, and a vintage label from the legendary Fairmont Hotel are eclectic mementos of this charming City by the Bay.

SAN FRANCISCO FROM THE PACIFIC

SAN FRANCISCO

CALIFORNIA

GOLDEN GATE BRIDGE
SAN FRANCISCO
CALIFORNIA

SAN FRANCISCO

SAN FRANCISCO

SAN FRANCISCO
NOV.
24
1912
AVIATION POST OFFICE

SAN FRANCISCO

Cabinet drawer of San Francisco–related postcards, covers, and decals.

Map of San
Francisco,
including other
tourist items, 1909.

Facing:
Brochure and
map of Golden
Gate Bridge and
Redwoods, 1948.

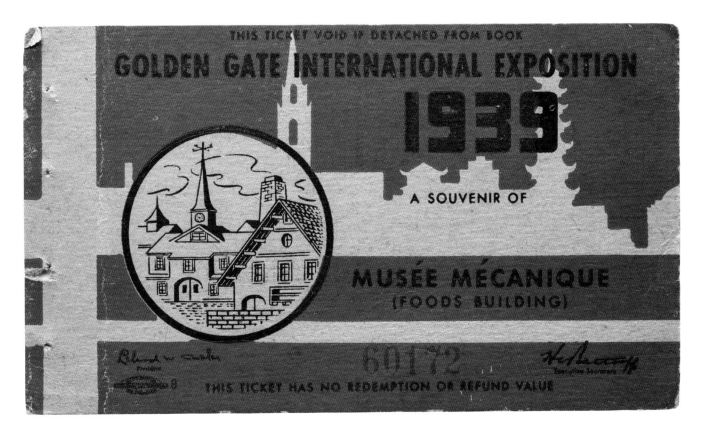

Facing:
Cover *USS Bridge*
for opening day of
Golden Gate Bridge,
postmarked from Mare
Island to Pasadena,
CA, on May 27, 1937.

Souvenir box cover of
Golden Gate Bridge
catwalk, 1937.

This page:
Label for San Francisco
World's Fair, 1939.

Ticket for Sutro
Baths, San Francisco,
circa 1900.

Ticket for Golden
Gate International
Exposition, Musée
Mécanique, 1939.

Poster stamp for San Francisco–Oakland Bay Bridge by Associated Oil Company, 1938.

Poster stamp for Golden Gate International Exposition, 1939.

Decal of San Francisco's Fisherman Wharf for car window or luggage, 1951.

Facing: Collection of San Francisco souvenirs, 20th century.

Facing:
Technical booklet
for San Francisco–
Oakland Bay
Bridge, 1935.

This page:
Decal of Oakland
Bay Bridge, 1951,
housed in library
card catalog.

SAN FRANCISCO
CALIF.

SOUVENIR OF San Francisco CALIF.

FERRY BLDG AND BAY

SAN FRANCISCO

THE QUALITY CITY

Greetings from SAN FRANCISCO CALIF.

© STANLEY A. PILTZ

Souvenir pennant of Ferry Building and bay, San Francisco, date unknown.

Postcard Greetings from San Francisco, 1941.

Foil poster stamp of San Francisco, The Quality City, circa 1939.

Decal of San Francisco's Chinatown for car window or luggage, 1951, placed on San Francisco City Directory, 1955.

SOUVENIR DECALS 10c
EASY TO APPLY WITH WATER
COIT TOWER
SAN FRANCISCO CALIF.
for Car windows • Collectors • Luggage

First Edition
18   5 4 3

Text © 2014 Brian D. Coleman
Photographs © 2014 William Wright

Published by
Gibbs Smith
P.O. Box 667
Layton, Utah 84041

1.800.835.4993 orders
www.gibbs-smith.com

Cover designed by Jennifer Chen, Cavallini & Co.
Interiors designed by Kurt Hauser
Printed and bound in China

Gibbs Smith books are printed on either
recycled, 100% post-consumer waste, FSC-
certified papers or on paper produced from
sustainable PEFC-certified forest/controlled
wood source. Learn more at www.pefc.org.

Library of Congress Control Number: 2014937041

ISBN 13: 978-1-4236-3364-8

John Ellison
1899

8
40   1 40
20
41
03   41   20
3
28   42   10

R ISLIP
KETTERING
No 0294

R WINDSOR
CASTLE
No 0780

EXPRÈS
EKSPRESS

3   Nov. 18

POSTAGE ONE PENNY

ONE PENNY

POSTAGE ONE

POSTAGE ONE

197

629

POSTAGE REVENUE   1½ POSTAGE REVENUE
ONE PENNY   THREE HALFPENCE

EXPRÈS

ONDON E.C. C
764074

ONE PENNY

(Nord)

... lettre ce matin ...
... les douleurs, recevez en ...
... les ... amenera
... la guerie ...
... contente de recevoir ...
... bonne santé ...
... le vilain ...
... allons ...
... nous embrassez affectueusement

CARTE POSTALE
Tous les Pays étrangers n'acceptent pas la Correspondance au recto.
(Se renseigner à la Poste)

CORRESPONDANCE — ADRESSE

le 27 Juillet 09

Monsieur et Madame
Ricaud Augustin
propriétaire quartier de
la terrasse — à
Robion — Vaucluse

CARTE POSTALE
Tous les Pays étrangers n'acceptent pas la Correspondance au recto.
(Se renseigner à la Poste)

CORRESPONDANCE — ADRESSE

Un bonjour
de Madame Martin

Madame Foissier
à Condé Ste Libiaire
par Esbly
Seine et Marne

P. Foissin

TIMBRE

POSTALE

CARTE POSTALE